Unleash Your Inner Entrepreneur: The Power of the Growth Mindset

Engin Yokaribas

DEDICATION

To Mini and Maxi,

My faithful companions, my bundles of joy, and my constant source of peace of mind. You two adorable bunnies have brought immense happiness and serenity into my life. Your playful antics, gentle nature, and unconditional love have been a source of comfort and solace during the journey of writing this book.

In moments of doubt and frustration, you were always there, hopping around, reminding me to find joy in the simple things and to embrace each day with enthusiasm. Your presence has been a reminder to live in the present moment, to appreciate the beauty of nature, and to find peace in the smallest of pleasures.

Through your innocent eyes, I have learned the importance of nurturing relationships, caring for others, and embracing the power of companionship. You have taught me the value of patience, as I watched you explore and discover the world around you at your own pace.

CONTENTS

	Introduction	1
1	What is an Entrepreneur?	Pg 5
2	Breaking Free from Self-Limiting Thoughts	Pg 9
3	Humor is the Hustle	Pg 18
4	Embracing Change and Adaptability	Pg 27
5	Building Resilience: Bouncing Back from Challenges	Pg 37
6	Cultivating Persistence: Staying the Course	Pg 48
7	Nurturing a Culture of Innovation	Pg 58
8	Embracing Collaboration	Pg 69
	Conclusion	Pg 80
	About the Author	Pg 85

INTRODUCTION

Welcome to the world of limitless possibilities and boundless growth! In "Unleash Your Inner Entrepreneur: The Power of the Growth Mindset," we embark on a transformative journey that will revolutionize the way you approach business and unlock your true potential as an entrepreneur.

In today's dynamic and ever-evolving business landscape, a strong mindset is the driving force behind success. It is the foundation upon which great achievements are built, and it sets apart those who thrive from those who merely survive. The growth mindset, in particular, holds the key to unleashing your inner entrepreneur and propelling you towards extraordinary accomplishments.

So, what exactly is the growth mindset? Coined by renowned psychologist Carol Dweck, the growth mindset is a belief system that emphasizes the power of effort, learning, and resilience in achieving success. It is the understanding that our abilities and talents can be developed through dedication, practice, and a willingness to embrace challenges.

In the pages of this book, we will dive deep into the core principles of the growth mindset and explore how it can revolutionize your entrepreneurial journey. By adopting a growth mindset, you will cultivate a mindset that thrives on continuous learning, embraces setbacks as opportunities for growth, and embraces the notion that failure is not a permanent state but rather a stepping stone towards success.

Throughout this exhilarating adventure, we will encounter real-life examples of Forbes 500 entrepreneurs who have embodied the growth mindset and harnessed its power to build empires. Their stories will serve as beacons of inspiration, demonstrating how a simple shift in mindset can lead to remarkable achievements and open doors to previously unimagined possibilities.

But why is mindset so crucial in the world of entrepreneurship? The answer lies in the unique challenges that entrepreneurs face. Building and growing a business demands resilience, adaptability, creativity, and a hunger for continuous improvement. It requires the ability to navigate uncertainty, embrace risks, and persevere in the face of obstacles.

By cultivating a growth mindset, you will develop the mental fortitude necessary to conquer these challenges head-on. You will transform setbacks into stepping stones, viewing failures as valuable lessons rather than insurmountable roadblocks. With a growth mindset, you will approach challenges with curiosity and a willingness to learn, leading to innovative solutions and groundbreaking ideas.

Moreover, the growth mindset fosters a sense of empowerment and ownership over your own success. It reminds you that you are not bound by your current abilities or circumstances but rather have the capacity to grow, adapt, and achieve greatness. It is an invitation to step outside your comfort zone, embrace change, and embrace the vast opportunities that lie before you.

Throughout this book, we will explore practical strategies and actionable tips to cultivate and strengthen your growth mindset. We will delve into the power of reframing self-limiting beliefs, infusing humor into the hustle, embracing resilience and adaptability, unleashing creativity and innovation, seizing entrepreneurial opportunities, nurturing a hunger for continuous learning, and building resilient networks and support systems.

Get ready to embark on a laughter-filled, eye-opening, and life-changing journey. The path to unleashing your inner entrepreneur begins here. Together, let us unravel the transformative power of the growth mindset and embark on a remarkable adventure that will propel you towards unparalleled success.

So, fasten your seatbelts, grab a cup of coffee, and get ready to unleash your inner entrepreneur. The power of the growth mindset awaits, and your journey to greatness starts now. Let's dive in!

1 WHAT IS AN ENTREPRENEUR

"The entrepreneur always searches for change, responds to it, and exploits it as an opportunity." - Peter F. Drucker

Entrepreneurship is a term often used in business and economic contexts, but what does it truly mean to be an entrepreneur? Is it solely about starting a business or taking risks? While these elements are certainly part of the entrepreneurial journey, being an entrepreneur encompasses much more. In this chapter, we will explore the essence of entrepreneurship and shed light on the characteristics and qualities that define an entrepreneur.

At its core, an entrepreneur is a visionary, someone who has a unique ability to identify opportunities and transform them into viable ventures. Entrepreneurs possess a remarkable combination of traits that set them apart from others. They are driven by a passion for innovation, an unwavering belief in their ideas, and a determination to bring their visions to life. They are risk-takers, willing to step out of their comfort zones and embrace uncertainty in pursuit of their goals.

However, being an entrepreneur is not solely about individual ambition and success. Entrepreneurs also possess a keen sense of empathy and a desire to create value for others. They understand that true success comes from solving problems, meeting needs, and making a positive impact on society. Whether it's through creating innovative products, offering unique services, or implementing groundbreaking solutions, entrepreneurs are driven by a sense of purpose and a desire to make a difference.

Entrepreneurship comes in many forms, and it is not limited to traditional business ventures. While some entrepreneurs may embark on the path of starting and scaling a company, others may focus on social entrepreneurship, aiming to address social or environmental challenges through sustainable business models. There are also tech entrepreneurs who leverage technology and digital platforms to disrupt industries and transform the way we live and work. Regardless of the specific focus, what unites all entrepreneurs is their ability to see beyond the status quo and imagine a better future.

Successful entrepreneurs possess a set of key qualities and skills that enable them to navigate the challenges and complexities of the entrepreneurial journey. They are highly adaptable, able to pivot and adjust their strategies in response to changing market dynamics. They are resilient, bouncing back from setbacks and failures with renewed determination. They are also excellent problem solvers, using their creativity and resourcefulness to find innovative solutions to the challenges they encounter.

Entrepreneurs are lifelong learners, constantly seeking new knowledge and skills to stay ahead of the curve. They are not afraid to ask for help or seek guidance from mentors and advisors. They understand the importance of building a strong network and surrounding themselves with talented individuals who complement their own skills and expertise.

It is important to note that entrepreneurship is not limited to a select few. Anyone with the right mindset, passion, and dedication can embark on the entrepreneurial journey. While some may have a natural inclination towards entrepreneurship, others can develop the necessary skills and mindset over time. It is a journey of continuous growth and self-discovery, where every challenge and setback becomes an opportunity for learning and improvement.

Examples of notable entrepreneurs abound, from Elon Musk and Oprah Winfrey to Mark Zuckerberg and Sara Blakely. Each of them has carved their own unique path, defying the odds and making a significant impact in their respective fields. Their stories serve as inspiration and a reminder that entrepreneurship is not limited by age, background, or circumstances. It is a mindset, a way of thinking and approaching the world with curiosity, creativity, and a relentless drive to make things happen.

In conclusion, being an entrepreneur is not just about starting a business or taking risks. It is a mindset, a way of life characterized by vision, passion, resilience, and a commitment to making a positive impact. Entrepreneurs are the catalysts for change, the drivers of innovation, and the builders of a better future. Whether you are already on the entrepreneurial path or considering taking the leap, embrace the qualities of an entrepreneur, nurture your mindset, and let your entrepreneurial journey become a transformative force in your life and the lives of others.

2 BREAKING FREE FROM SELF-LIMITING BELIEFS

"Whether you think you can or you think you can't, you're right." - Henry Ford

Welcome to the second chapter of "Unleash Your Inner Entrepreneur: The Power of the Growth Mindset." In this chapter, we delve deep into the transformative process of breaking free from self-limiting beliefs and embracing the growth mindset. By understanding and challenging these beliefs, you will unlock the true potential within you and set the stage for remarkable entrepreneurial success.

UNDERSTANDING SELF-LIMITING BELIEFS

Understanding self-limiting beliefs is an essential step in cultivating a growth mindset. These beliefs often stem from past experiences, societal messages, or negative self-talk that create doubt and hinder our progress. However, it's important to remember that self-limiting beliefs are not based on objective truth but rather on our own perceptions and interpretations.

To overcome self-limiting beliefs, we need to challenge and reframe them. Start by questioning the validity of these beliefs. Is there any real evidence to support them? Often, these beliefs are based on assumptions or past failures, rather than concrete facts. Look for counterexamples and success stories that prove your self-limiting beliefs wrong.

Consider how these beliefs serve you. Do they empower and motivate you, or do they hold you back from taking risks and pursuing your goals? Recognize that clinging to self-limiting beliefs limits your potential for growth and success. By letting go of these beliefs, you open yourself up to new possibilities and opportunities.

Replace self-limiting beliefs with more empowering and growth-oriented thoughts. Instead of saying, "I'm not smart enough," reframe it as, "I have the ability to learn and acquire the knowledge necessary for success." Challenge the belief that failure is inevitable by embracing the idea that failure is a natural part of the learning process and an opportunity for growth.

It's important to remember that overcoming self-limiting beliefs is an ongoing process. Be patient and kind to yourself as you work on shifting your mindset. Surround yourself with positive influences, such as supportive mentors, like-minded peers, or inspiring role models who have overcome similar beliefs and achieved success.

By actively challenging and reframing self-limiting beliefs, you can create a mental environment that fosters growth, resilience, and confidence. This will enable you to approach challenges with a positive mindset, embrace learning opportunities, and strive for continuous improvement.

Remember, you have the power to shape your beliefs and mindset. By letting go of self-limiting beliefs and embracing a growth mindset, you open yourself up to endless possibilities and pave the way for entrepreneurial success.

THE POWER OF THE GROWTH MINDSET

The power of the growth mindset lies in its ability to transform the way we approach challenges, setbacks, and personal growth. Entrepreneurs who embrace a growth mindset understand that their abilities are not fixed but can be developed and expanded through effort and dedication.

With a growth mindset, entrepreneurs view failures and setbacks as valuable learning opportunities. They don't see them as indications of their worth or intelligence but as stepping stones on the path to success. Instead of being discouraged by obstacles, they approach them with resilience, determination, and a belief that they can learn from their experiences and improve.

Entrepreneurs with a growth mindset also prioritize continuous learning and personal growth. They understand that success is not just about reaching a specific goal but about the journey of self-improvement. They actively seek out new knowledge, skills, and experiences that can enhance their entrepreneurial abilities and enable them to adapt to a rapidly changing business landscape.

By embracing a growth mindset, entrepreneurs develop a more positive and optimistic outlook on their entrepreneurial endeavors. They see challenges as opportunities to stretch their abilities and develop new skills. This mindset fosters a sense of curiosity, creativity, and a willingness to take calculated risks.

The growth mindset also empowers entrepreneurs to persevere in the face of adversity. Instead of giving up when faced with obstacles, they approach them with determination and a belief that they can find solutions. They understand that setbacks are not permanent roadblocks but temporary hurdles that can be overcome through perseverance and innovative thinking.

Entrepreneurs who cultivate a growth mindset also understand the value of feedback and constructive criticism. They seek out mentors, advisors, and peers who can provide them with valuable insights and guidance. They are open to receiving feedback, as they see it as an opportunity for growth and improvement.

Moreover, the growth mindset encourages entrepreneurs to embrace collaboration and surround themselves with like-minded individuals who share their passion for growth and learning. They understand that by leveraging the collective knowledge, skills, and experiences of others, they can accelerate their own growth and achieve greater success.

In summary, the power of the growth mindset lies in its ability to transform entrepreneurs' approach to challenges, setbacks, and personal growth. By embracing a growth mindset, entrepreneurs can overcome self-limiting beliefs, view failures as learning opportunities, prioritize continuous learning, persevere in the face of adversity, and harness the power of collaboration. With a growth mindset, entrepreneurs can unlock their full potential and achieve remarkable success in their entrepreneurial endeavors.

REAL-LIFE EXAMPLES OF FORBES 500 ENTREPRENEURS

Let's draw inspiration from the stories of Forbes 500 entrepreneurs who have shattered self-limiting beliefs and harnessed the power of the growth mindset to achieve extraordinary success:

1. Elon Musk, CEO of Tesla and SpaceX: Elon Musk's journey is a testament to the power of belief in one's vision and the audacity to challenge the status quo. Despite facing numerous setbacks, including rocket launch failures and skepticism from industry experts, Musk persisted with an unwavering belief in his ability to revolutionize the electric car and space exploration industries.

2. Oprah Winfrey, Media Mogul and Philanthropist: Oprah Winfrey's rise to success is a testament to the triumph over personal and societal barriers. Coming from a challenging background, she faced gender and racial discrimination. However, she refused to let these circumstances define her. Through her determination, resilience, and unwavering belief in her own potential, she built an empire and became one of the most influential media figures in history.

3. Jeff Bezos, Founder of Amazon: Jeff Bezos demonstrated a growth mindset by constantly challenging himself and embracing a long-term perspective. Despite starting Amazon as an online bookstore, Bezos had a grand vision of transforming it into a global e-commerce giant. He consistently pushed boundaries, expanded into new markets, and took calculated risks, always believing in the potential for growth and innovation.

OVERCOMING SELF-LIMITING BELIEFS

Now that we understand the power of the growth mindset through these remarkable examples, it's time to explore strategies to overcome self-limiting beliefs and cultivate a mindset of growth:

1. Awareness and Reflection: The first step is to become aware of your self-limiting beliefs. Take time to reflect on the thoughts and beliefs that may be holding you back. Recognize that these beliefs are not absolute truths but rather conditioned perceptions that can be challenged and changed.

2. Challenging Negative Self-Talk: Replace self-limiting thoughts with positive and empowering affirmations. When negative self-talk arises, consciously counter it with statements like, "I am capable of learning and growing," or "I embrace challenges as opportunities for growth."

3. Embrace the Power of Yet: Instead of saying, "I can't do this," add the word "yet" to the end of the sentence. For example, "I can't do this...yet." This simple addition opens up possibilities and reminds you that growth and progress take time and effort.

4. Embrace Failure as a Stepping Stone: Shift your perspective on failure from a negative outcome to a valuable learning experience. Embrace failures as opportunities for growth and improvement, viewing them as stepping stones on your path to success.

5. Surround Yourself with Positive Influences: Seek out mentors, role models, and supportive peers who embody the growth mindset. Their positive influence and belief in your abilities will help reinforce your own self-belief and encourage your entrepreneurial journey.

CONCLUSION

In conclusion, breaking free from self-limiting beliefs is a transformative step on your journey to becoming an empowered entrepreneur. By embracing the growth mindset and challenging these beliefs, you unlock a world of boundless possibilities and untapped potential. The stories of Forbes 500 entrepreneurs serve as powerful reminders that our beliefs shape our reality, and by adopting a growth mindset, we can surpass our own expectations and achieve remarkable success.

The journey towards embracing a growth mindset is not always easy, but it is worth the effort. It requires self-reflection, awareness, and a willingness to challenge the beliefs that have held you back. As you embark on this journey, remember that you have the power to shape your own reality. Your mindset is not fixed; it can be developed, nurtured, and expanded.

Let go of the self-imposed limitations that have hindered your progress and embrace the growth mindset with open arms. Believe in your ability to learn, adapt, and grow as an entrepreneur. Embrace failure as a stepping stone to success and view setbacks as opportunities for growth and improvement.

As you continue on your entrepreneurial path, surround yourself with a supportive network of mentors, peers, and role models who share your passion for growth and development. Seek out collaboration and feedback, and never stop learning from the experiences of others.

Remember that your mindset is a powerful force that can propel you towards greatness. It is the foundation upon which you will build your entrepreneurial journey. Embrace the power of the growth mindset and let it guide your thoughts, actions, and decisions.

Now is the time to unleash your inner entrepreneur, armed with the transformative power of the growth mindset. Embrace the challenges, celebrate the milestones, and let your entrepreneurial endeavors leave a lasting impact on the world. The power to transform your mindset and achieve greatness is within your grasp. Believe in it, embrace it, and let it propel you towards extraordinary achievements.

The journey towards entrepreneurial triumph starts with a single step – the decision to cultivate a growth mindset. So, take that step, break free from self-limiting beliefs, and unleash your inner entrepreneur. Your potential knows no bounds. The world awaits your brilliance, your innovation, and your unwavering belief in the power of growth. Embrace the journey, celebrate the milestones, and let your entrepreneurial spirit soar. The future is yours for the taking.

3 HUMOR IN THE HUSTLE

"A sense of humor is part of the art of leadership, of getting along with people, of getting things done." - Dwight D. Eisenhower

Welcome to Chapter 3 of "Unleash Your Inner Entrepreneur: The Power of the Growth Mindset." In this chapter, we delve into the transformative role of humor in entrepreneurship. We explore how humor can not only alleviate the stresses and challenges of the entrepreneurial journey but also enhance problem-solving skills and foster a positive mindset. Get ready to discover the remarkable benefits of infusing humor into your hustle and unlock the power of laughter on your path to success.

THE POWER OF HUMOR

The power of humor cannot be underestimated, especially in the context of entrepreneurship. Humor serves as a universal language that brings people together and breaks down barriers. It has a remarkable ability to lighten the mood, shift perspectives, and create connections. When used effectively, humor can become a powerful tool for navigating the challenges and uncertainties that arise on the path to entrepreneurial success.

Entrepreneurs who incorporate humor into their daily lives and businesses experience numerous benefits. One of the key advantages is its ability to help maintain a positive mindset. Entrepreneurship is filled with ups and downs, and the ability to find humor in difficult situations can provide a much-needed perspective shift. It allows entrepreneurs to see challenges as opportunities for growth and keeps them motivated even in the face of adversity.

Moreover, humor fosters creativity and innovation. By infusing humor into the creative process, entrepreneurs can break free from conventional thinking and explore new possibilities. Humor opens the door to unconventional ideas, encouraging out-of-the-box thinking and promoting a culture of innovation within the business.

In addition to enhancing creativity, humor also plays a crucial role in building stronger relationships. It creates a sense of camaraderie among team members, encourages collaboration, and fosters a positive work environment. When humor is embraced, it helps to alleviate stress and tension, allowing for better communication and increased productivity. Customers also appreciate a lighthearted and humorous approach, as it creates a memorable and enjoyable experience.

Beyond the business realm, humor has significant benefits for overall well-being. It has been proven to reduce stress, boost mood, and improve overall mental and emotional health. Entrepreneurs face high levels of stress and pressure, and incorporating humor into their lives acts as a coping mechanism. It enables them to take a step back, find moments of joy, and maintain a healthy work-life balance.

The power of humor lies not only in its ability to bring joy and laughter but also in its impact on mindset and perspective. It helps entrepreneurs develop a growth mindset by allowing them to embrace failures and setbacks with a lighter heart. It encourages them to approach challenges with resilience and a positive attitude. By infusing humor into their businesses, entrepreneurs create an environment that nurtures innovation, collaboration, and personal growth.

In summary, the power of humor in entrepreneurship is undeniable. It serves as a catalyst for maintaining a positive mindset, fostering creativity, building strong relationships, and promoting overall well-being. By infusing humor into the entrepreneurial journey, entrepreneurs can create a culture that embraces innovation, resilience, and a growth mindset. So, let laughter be the fuel that propels you forward on your entrepreneurial path, and remember that a smile can be the key to unlocking your true potential.

REAL-LIFE EXAMPLES OF FORBES 500 ENTREPRENEURS

Let's draw inspiration from the stories of Forbes 500 entrepreneurs who have embraced humor and used it as a catalyst for success:

1. Richard Branson, Founder of Virgin Group: Richard Branson is known for his playful and light-hearted approach to business. He infuses humor into the Virgin brand, creating a fun and engaging experience for customers. His willingness to take risks and inject humor into various aspects of his ventures has helped him stand out in competitive industries and build a loyal customer base.

2. Sara Blakely, Founder of Spanx: Sara Blakely's journey to success is filled with humorous anecdotes. She often shares stories of her early struggles and failures, injecting humor into the challenges she faced. Blakely's ability to find laughter in adversity not only helped her

maintain a positive mindset but also allowed her to connect with others on a relatable level.

3. Reed Hastings, Co-founder of Netflix: Reed Hastings is known for his witty and humorous approach to leadership. He incorporates humor into company culture and embraces the power of laughter to foster creativity and collaboration among team members. Hastings understands that a lighthearted environment can lead to more innovative ideas and a stronger sense of camaraderie within the organization.

THE BENEFITS OF HUMOR IN THE ENTREPRENEURIAL JOURNEY

Now, let's explore the specific benefits of infusing humor into your hustle:

1. Stress Relief: The entrepreneurial journey is often accompanied by high levels of stress. Humor serves as a natural stress reliever, helping you navigate challenges with a lighter perspective. It releases endorphins, reduces tension, and improves overall well-being, allowing you to approach obstacles with a clearer mind and increased resilience.

2. Creative Problem-Solving: Humor stimulates creativity and divergent thinking. When you engage in playful and humorous thinking, you break free from rigid thought patterns and open yourself up to unconventional solutions. It encourages outside-the-box thinking, leading to innovative problem-solving and unique business strategies.

3. Building Resilience: Humor cultivates a resilient mindset by helping you reframe setbacks and failures. Instead of dwelling on negative outcomes, you can find humor in the situation, learn from it, and move forward. It allows you to bounce back more quickly, adapt to changes, and maintain a positive outlook, even in challenging times.

4. Enhanced Communication and Collaboration: Humor promotes open communication, breaks down barriers, and strengthens relationships. When you use humor in your interactions with team members, employees, and customers, you create a positive and engaging atmosphere. It fosters stronger connections, encourages collaboration, and improves overall teamwork.

5. Customer Engagement and Loyalty: Incorporating humor into your marketing and customer interactions creates memorable experiences. Humor can make your brand relatable, approachable, and stand out from competitors. It builds a genuine connection with your audience, leading to increased customer engagement, loyalty, and word-of-mouth referrals.

HOW TO INFUSE HUMOR INTO YOUR HUSTLE

Now that we understand the benefits, let's explore practical strategies for infusing humor into your entrepreneurial journey:

1. Embrace Lightheartedness: Adopt a lighthearted and playful attitude towards your work. Find joy in the process, celebrate small wins, and don't be afraid to laugh at yourself along the way.

2. Incorporate Humor in Marketing and Branding: Use humor to create memorable marketing campaigns, social media content, and branding initiatives. Injecting wit and humor into your messaging can make your brand more relatable and appealing to your target audience.

3. Create a Positive and Fun Work Environment: Foster a culture that encourages humor and laughter within your team. Organize team-building activities, share funny stories, and create a space where people feel comfortable expressing their sense of humor.

4. Embrace Playfulness in Problem-Solving: When faced with challenges, approach them with a playful mindset. Encourage brainstorming sessions where humor is welcomed, and encourage your team to explore unconventional ideas without fear of judgment.

5. Learn from Comedians and Improvisation: Study the techniques of comedians and improvisation performers. They excel at thinking on their feet, finding humor in unexpected situations, and creating connections with their audience. Incorporate their techniques into your presentations, pitches, and public speaking engagements.

CONCLUSION

In conclusion, humor is not just a luxury or a frivolous indulgence; it is a powerful ally on your entrepreneurial journey. By infusing humor into the hustle and bustle of business, you can reap numerous benefits that contribute to your success.

One of the key advantages of humor is its ability to alleviate stress. As an entrepreneur, you face high levels of pressure, uncertainty, and demanding challenges. Humor acts as a release valve, allowing you to find moments of lightness and joy amidst the chaos. It brings a sense of perspective, reminding you that not everything needs to be taken so seriously. By finding humor in the face of adversity, you can maintain a more balanced and resilient mindset.

Moreover, humor fosters creativity. It encourages you to think outside the box, challenge conventions, and explore new possibilities. When you infuse humor into your creative process, it opens up pathways to innovative solutions and novel approaches. Humor allows you to connect seemingly unrelated ideas, leading to fresh insights and breakthroughs in your business endeavors.

Building strong relationships is another powerful outcome of incorporating humor into your entrepreneurial journey. Laughter creates bonds and breaks down barriers between people. It creates a positive and enjoyable work environment where team members feel comfortable expressing their ideas and collaborating. Humor helps to build trust, strengthen communication, and foster a sense of camaraderie. It also resonates with customers, as it enhances their experience and makes your brand more memorable.

Beyond its impact on business, humor has significant benefits for your overall well-being. It reduces stress, boosts mood, and improves your mental and emotional health. By finding moments of laughter and joy, you can better manage the inevitable ups and downs of entrepreneurship. Taking the time to appreciate the lighter side of life enhances your work-life balance, promotes self-care, and contributes to your long-term success.

The stories of Forbes 500 entrepreneurs serve as powerful reminders that humor is not a distraction from success but a catalyst for it. These successful individuals have embraced the power of laughter and playfulness in their entrepreneurial journeys. They understand that humor can be a driving force behind creativity, resilience, and a positive mindset. By embracing humor, they have achieved remarkable success while also enjoying the journey.

So, as you conclude your reading of this book, remember to embrace humor as a valuable tool in your entrepreneurial toolkit. Laugh in the face of challenges, find joy in the process, and let humor infuse every aspect of your business and personal life. Embracing the transformative power of laughter will not only make your entrepreneurial journey more enjoyable but will also unlock new levels of creativity, resilience, and success.

In the end, it's not just about building a successful business; it's about creating a life of fulfillment and happiness. So, embrace humor, find the funny side of life, and let laughter be your constant companion on the path to entrepreneurial greatness.

4 EMBRACING CHANGE AND ADAPTABILITY

"Adaptability is not about changing who you are, but rather adjusting your sails to navigate the winds of change." - Brian Tracy

Welcome to Chapter 4 of "Unleash Your Inner Entrepreneur: The Power of the Growth Mindset." In this chapter, we explore the critical role of embracing change and adaptability in entrepreneurial success. The business landscape is constantly evolving, and those who can navigate and embrace change have a distinct advantage. By cultivating a growth mindset that embraces change and fosters adaptability, you can position yourself for long-term success in the dynamic world of entrepreneurship.

THE NATURE OF CHANGE IN ENTREPRENEURSHIP

Change is not just a possibility but an unavoidable reality in the world of entrepreneurship. The very nature of entrepreneurship demands adaptability and a willingness to embrace change. From shifting market trends and technological advancements to evolving consumer preferences and competitive landscapes, entrepreneurs must be prepared to navigate a rapidly changing environment.

Resisting change is a risky endeavor. Clinging to outdated strategies and refusing to evolve can lead to stagnation and irrelevance. In a world where innovation and disruption are the norm, it is essential for entrepreneurs to recognize that change is not their enemy but an opportunity for growth and success.

Entrepreneurs who embrace change understand that it is a catalyst for progress. They view change as a chance to uncover new possibilities, explore untapped markets, and create innovative solutions. By staying attuned to industry trends and consumer needs, they can proactively respond to changing dynamics and position themselves for long-term success.

One of the key attributes of successful entrepreneurs is their ability to anticipate and leverage change. They are constantly scanning the horizon, seeking opportunities for innovation and improvement. Rather than fearing change, they embrace it as a means to disrupt the status quo and create value for their customers.

In the face of change, entrepreneurs must be agile and adaptable. They must be willing to pivot their strategies, adjust their business models, and even reinvent themselves when necessary. This requires a mindset of continuous learning and a willingness to step outside of comfort zones. Entrepreneurs who are open to change are better equipped to seize emerging opportunities and navigate challenges with resilience.

It's important to note that change is not always easy. It can be disruptive, challenging, and even uncomfortable. However, successful entrepreneurs recognize that the rewards of embracing change far outweigh the risks. They understand that change is not a one-time event but an ongoing process. By cultivating a mindset that embraces change, entrepreneurs position themselves as leaders in their industries, capable of driving innovation and staying ahead of the curve.

The stories of Forbes 500 entrepreneurs highlight the significance of embracing change. These successful individuals have not only adapted to change but have thrived in dynamic and evolving markets. They have embraced new technologies, disrupted traditional industries, and created groundbreaking products and services. Their journeys serve as inspiration for aspiring entrepreneurs, showcasing the power of embracing change as a pathway to success.

In conclusion, change is an inherent part of the entrepreneurial journey. Entrepreneurs who resist change or cling to outdated strategies risk being left behind. However, those who embrace change as an opportunity can thrive. By staying attuned to market dynamics, anticipating trends, and being willing to adapt, entrepreneurs can position themselves for long-term success. Embracing change requires agility, resilience, and a growth mindset. It may not always be easy, but the rewards are worth the effort. So, as you embark on your entrepreneurial journey, embrace change as a catalyst for growth and innovation. Let it propel you forward and open doors to new and exciting possibilities.

THE GROWTH MINDSET AND ADAPTABILITY

Adaptability is a key characteristic of successful entrepreneurs, and at the heart of adaptability lies the growth mindset. The growth mindset is a belief that talents, abilities, and intelligence can be developed through dedication, effort, and continuous learning. Entrepreneurs who embrace the growth mindset understand that change is not a threat but a gateway to new possibilities and growth opportunities.

Entrepreneurs with a growth mindset see challenges and setbacks as valuable learning experiences. They view obstacles as temporary roadblocks that can be overcome with the right mindset and strategies. Rather than being discouraged by failure, they see it as an opportunity to grow, learn, and improve. They understand that their abilities are not fixed, but can be developed over time through deliberate practice and a commitment to continuous learning.

The growth mindset enables entrepreneurs to adapt to changing circumstances with ease. They are open to new ideas, willing to experiment, and embrace feedback as a means of improvement. Instead of being confined by their comfort zones, they actively seek out opportunities to stretch themselves and expand their skills. They understand that adaptation is a necessary part of the entrepreneurial journey and are willing to evolve their strategies and approaches as needed.

Entrepreneurs with a growth mindset also possess a strong sense of resilience. They are not easily deterred by setbacks or obstacles. Instead, they approach challenges with a positive attitude, perseverance, and a belief that they can overcome any hurdle. They understand that setbacks are not indicators of permanent failure, but stepping stones on the path to success.

The growth mindset also encourages entrepreneurs to embrace lifelong learning. They recognize that knowledge and skills are not finite resources but can be continuously expanded. They seek out opportunities for personal and professional growth, whether it's through reading books, attending workshops, or seeking mentorship. They understand that staying relevant and competitive in a rapidly changing business landscape requires a commitment to ongoing learning and self-improvement.

The stories of Forbes 500 entrepreneurs exemplify the power of the growth mindset and adaptability. These individuals have not only achieved remarkable success but have also faced numerous challenges and setbacks along the way. However, their ability to embrace the growth mindset and adapt to changing circumstances has allowed them to thrive in dynamic and competitive markets.

In conclusion, the growth mindset and adaptability go hand in hand in the entrepreneurial journey. Entrepreneurs with a growth mindset understand that change is an opportunity for growth and improvement. They are resilient in the face of challenges, open to new ideas, and committed to continuous learning. By embracing the growth mindset, entrepreneurs position themselves to navigate the ever-changing business landscape with agility and success. So, cultivate a growth mindset, embrace change, and let adaptability be your guiding force on the path to entrepreneurial greatness.

REAL-LIFE EXAMPLES OF FORBES 500 ENTREPRENEURS

Let's draw inspiration from the stories of Forbes 500 entrepreneurs who have exemplified the power of embracing change and adaptability:

1. Satya Nadella, CEO of Microsoft: Satya Nadella took the helm of Microsoft during a time when the company was struggling to keep up with the rapidly changing technology landscape. Instead of clinging to the status quo, Nadella embraced change and spearheaded a cultural shift within the organization. Under his leadership, Microsoft transitioned from a software-focused company to a cloud-based services provider, positioning itself for long-term success in the digital era.

2. Indra Nooyi, Former CEO of PepsiCo: Indra Nooyi led PepsiCo through a significant transformation to adapt to changing consumer

preferences and health trends. She recognized the growing demand for healthier food and beverages and steered the company towards diversifying its product portfolio to include healthier options. Nooyi's ability to adapt to shifting market dynamics and anticipate consumer needs helped PepsiCo maintain its competitive edge.

3. Brian Chesky, Co-founder of Airbnb: Brian Chesky demonstrated adaptability by recognizing the changing landscape of the travel industry. When faced with regulatory challenges and a shift in consumer behavior towards unique and personalized travel experiences, Chesky embraced change and transformed Airbnb from a platform for renting air mattresses to a global marketplace for unique accommodations. This adaptability allowed Airbnb to disrupt the hospitality industry and redefine the way people travel.

THE BENEFITS OF EMBRACING CHANGE AND ADAPTABILITY

Now, let's explore the specific benefits of embracing change and cultivating adaptability:

1. **Seizing New Opportunities**: Change brings new opportunities that can lead to business growth and success. By embracing change and being open to new possibilities, you position yourself to seize these opportunities and gain a competitive edge.

2. **Staying Ahead of the Curve**: In a rapidly evolving business landscape, adaptability allows you to stay ahead of the curve. By monitoring market trends, consumer behavior, and emerging technologies, you can proactively adapt your strategies and offerings to meet evolving needs and stay relevant.

3. Innovation and Creativity: Embracing change and adaptability fosters innovation and creativity. When faced with new challenges or changing circumstances, you are encouraged to think creatively, explore new solutions, and innovate within your industry.

4. Resilience in the Face of Adversity: Change often brings adversity and unexpected challenges. By embracing change and maintaining an adaptable mindset, you develop resilience and the ability to navigate through adversity with grace and determination.

5. Continuous Learning and Growth: Embracing change requires a willingness to learn and grow. By seeking new knowledge, acquiring new skills, and adapting to changing circumstances, you cultivate personal and professional growth that propels your entrepreneurial journey forward.

STRATEGIES FOR EMBRACING CHANGE AND CULTIVATING ADAPTABILITY

Now, let's explore practical strategies for embracing change and fostering adaptability in your entrepreneurial endeavors:

1. Embrace a Growth Mindset: Cultivate a growth mindset that embraces change as an opportunity for growth and improvement. Develop a belief in your ability to learn, adapt, and overcome challenges.

2. Foster a Culture of Adaptability: Create an organizational culture that values adaptability and encourages open communication, flexibility, and the willingness to embrace change. Encourage your team members to bring forward innovative ideas and solutions.

3. Stay Informed and Proactive: Stay updated on industry trends, market shifts, and technological advancements that could impact your business. Be proactive in anticipating and responding to these changes, rather than reacting when it's too late.

4. Embrace Lifelong Learning: Adopt a mindset of continuous learning. Seek out new knowledge, attend industry conferences, participate in workshops, and engage in networking opportunities to expand your skill set and stay ahead of the curve.

5. Seek Feedback and Learn from Failure: Embrace feedback as a valuable learning tool. Actively seek feedback from customers, mentors, and peers to gain insights and make necessary adjustments. Learn from failures and setbacks, using them as stepping stones for growth and improvement.

CONCLUSION

In conclusion, embracing change and cultivating adaptability are paramount for entrepreneurial success in today's rapidly evolving business landscape. By adopting a growth mindset and viewing change as an opportunity rather than a threat, you position yourself to seize new possibilities, stay ahead of the curve, and foster innovation.

Entrepreneurs who embrace change and cultivate adaptability are able to navigate the ever-shifting tides of the business world with agility and resilience. They understand that change is inevitable and that resisting it only hinders their progress. Instead, they choose to embrace change as a catalyst for growth and transformation.

By adopting a growth mindset, you recognize that your abilities and skills can be developed and improved over time. This mindset empowers you to approach challenges with a positive attitude, persevere through setbacks, and learn from failures. With a growth mindset, you view obstacles as stepping stones on the path to success, and you are willing to adapt your strategies and approaches as needed.

The stories of Forbes 500 entrepreneurs exemplify the power of embracing change and cultivating adaptability. These individuals have not only weathered the storms of uncertainty and disruption but have thrived in the face of adversity. Their success is a testament to the transformative potential of adaptability.

To become a truly adaptable entrepreneur, it is important to embrace a continuous learning mindset. Stay curious, seek out new knowledge, and be open to new ideas and perspectives. Engage in ongoing professional development, attend industry conferences, and surround yourself with a network of mentors and like-minded individuals who can inspire and challenge you.

Moreover, developing a strong support network is crucial for maintaining adaptability. Surround yourself with individuals who share your vision, believe in your potential, and support your growth. Collaborate with partners, team members, and mentors who can provide valuable insights and guidance during times of change.

As you embark on your entrepreneurial journey, remember that adaptability is not just about surviving change but thriving in it. Let go of the fear of the unknown and embrace change as an opportunity for growth and innovation. Cultivate a growth mindset, stay agile, and continuously seek new ways to evolve and improve.

In the dynamic world of entrepreneurship, those who are adaptable will have a competitive edge. So, let your adaptability become a superpower that propels you towards entrepreneurial greatness.

Embrace change, cultivate adaptability, and become the architect of your own success in the ever-changing business landscape.

5 BUILDING RESILIENCE: BOUNCING BACK FROM CHALLENGES

"The greatest glory in living lies not in never falling, but in rising every time we fall." - Nelson Mandela

Welcome to Chapter 5 of "Unleash Your Inner Entrepreneur: The Power of the Growth Mindset." In this chapter, we explore the importance of building resilience as an entrepreneur and how it can contribute to your long-term success. Resilience is the ability to bounce back from setbacks, adapt to adversity, and persevere in the face of challenges. By cultivating a growth mindset and developing resilience, you can navigate the ups and downs of the entrepreneurial journey with strength and determination.

THE ENTREPRENEURIAL ROLLERCOASTER

The entrepreneurial journey is often described as a rollercoaster ride, complete with thrilling highs and daunting lows. Success in entrepreneurship is seldom a straight and smooth path. Instead, it is filled with twists, turns, and unexpected loops that test the mettle of even the most determined individuals. To navigate this exhilarating yet challenging ride, entrepreneurs must possess a unique quality: resilience.

Resilience is the ability to bounce back from setbacks, adapt to change, and maintain a positive mindset in the face of adversity. It is the fuel that keeps entrepreneurs going when the going gets tough. During the lows of the entrepreneurial rollercoaster, resilience becomes a critical factor in determining an entrepreneur's ability to persevere and ultimately achieve their goals.

Challenges and obstacles are an inherent part of the entrepreneurial journey. Rejections, failures, financial struggles, and the fear of the unknown can all take their toll. However, resilient entrepreneurs view these setbacks as learning opportunities and stepping stones on the path to success. They understand that failure is not a permanent state but a temporary setback that provides valuable lessons and insights.

Resilient entrepreneurs maintain a positive mindset even in the face of adversity. They focus on the possibilities and opportunities that lie ahead rather than dwelling on past failures. They see challenges as tests of their strength and determination, pushing them to find innovative solutions and alternative paths to success.

The stories of Forbes 500 entrepreneurs highlight the importance of resilience on the entrepreneurial rollercoaster. These individuals have faced countless obstacles, experienced failures, and encountered setbacks. However, their ability to bounce back, learn from their experiences, and persevere has been instrumental in their ultimate success. Their stories serve as a reminder that resilience is not just a desirable trait but a necessary one for entrepreneurial greatness.

To cultivate resilience, entrepreneurs can take several steps. Firstly, it is important to develop a growth mindset. Embrace the belief that failures are learning opportunities and setbacks are temporary. Nurture a positive attitude and focus on the progress made rather than dwelling on setbacks.

Secondly, surround yourself with a supportive network. Seek out mentors, advisors, and fellow entrepreneurs who can provide guidance, encouragement, and a fresh perspective during challenging times. Collaboration and support can help alleviate the feelings of isolation and provide valuable insights and strategies for overcoming obstacles.

Thirdly, take care of your well-being. Entrepreneurship can be demanding and stressful, but it is crucial to prioritize self-care. Engage in activities that recharge your energy, whether it's exercising, spending time with loved ones, practicing mindfulness, or pursuing hobbies. By taking care of your physical and mental well-being, you can better navigate the ups and downs of the entrepreneurial rollercoaster.

In conclusion, resilience is the key to thriving on the entrepreneurial rollercoaster. The ability to bounce back from setbacks, adapt to change, and maintain a positive mindset is crucial for success. Embrace challenges as opportunities for growth, seek support from a strong network, and prioritize your well-being. Remember, the entrepreneurial journey is not for the faint of heart, but with resilience as your companion, you can ride the highs and conquer the lows on your path to entrepreneurial greatness.

THE GROWTH MINDSET AND RESILIENCE

Resilience and the growth mindset are intertwined in the entrepreneurial journey. Entrepreneurs who possess a growth mindset embrace setbacks and failures as stepping stones toward learning and growth, rather than seeing them as insurmountable roadblocks. They recognize that failure is not a reflection of their worth or abilities but a natural part of the path to success.

Entrepreneurs with a growth mindset approach challenges and setbacks with a different perspective. Instead of being discouraged by failures, they see them as valuable learning opportunities. They understand that each setback provides valuable insights, teaches important lessons, and offers a chance to improve and refine their strategies.

The growth mindset allows entrepreneurs to bounce back from setbacks with resilience and determination. They believe that their abilities and skills can be developed through dedication, effort, and continuous learning. This mindset enables them to maintain a positive outlook even in the face of adversity.

Resilient entrepreneurs understand that setbacks are not permanent. They view challenges as temporary roadblocks that can be overcome through perseverance, creative problem-solving, and adaptability. They are willing to embrace change, adjust their strategies, and explore new possibilities to overcome obstacles and move forward.

The stories of Forbes 500 entrepreneurs exemplify the connection between the growth mindset and resilience. These successful individuals have faced their fair share of failures and setbacks, but their growth mindset allowed them to persevere and ultimately achieve remarkable success. They embraced challenges, learned from their experiences, and used setbacks as opportunities to refine their approaches and propel themselves forward.

To cultivate resilience and a growth mindset, entrepreneurs can adopt several strategies. Firstly, it is important to reframe failures and setbacks as opportunities for growth and learning. Instead of dwelling on what went wrong, focus on the lessons learned and the skills gained from the experience.

Secondly, practice self-compassion. Recognize that setbacks are a natural part of the entrepreneurial journey and that it is okay to make mistakes. Treat yourself with kindness and understanding, and use setbacks as motivation to improve and grow.

Thirdly, surround yourself with a supportive network. Seek guidance and support from mentors, peers, and fellow entrepreneurs who can provide encouragement, share experiences, and offer valuable advice. Collaborating with others who have a growth mindset can inspire and uplift you during challenging times.

Additionally, take care of your well-being. Prioritize self-care, maintain a healthy work-life balance, and engage in activities that recharge your energy and foster a positive mindset. Remember that resilience is not just about overcoming obstacles; it is also about maintaining your physical and mental well-being to sustain your entrepreneurial journey.

In conclusion, the growth mindset and resilience go hand in hand on the entrepreneurial path. By embracing a growth mindset, entrepreneurs can view setbacks as opportunities for growth and learning. Resilience allows them to bounce back from failures and setbacks, adapt to challenges, and maintain a positive outlook. By cultivating a growth mindset and resilience, entrepreneurs can navigate the ups and downs of the entrepreneurial journey with confidence, perseverance, and a commitment to continuous growth.

REAL-LIFE EXAMPLES OF FORBES 500 ENTREPRENEURS

Let's draw inspiration from the stories of Forbes 500 entrepreneurs who have demonstrated resilience in the face of challenges:

1. Elon Musk, CEO of Tesla and SpaceX: Elon Musk's entrepreneurial journey has been marked by numerous challenges and setbacks. From rocket launch failures to production delays, Musk has faced adversity at every turn. However, he has consistently demonstrated resilience, bouncing back from setbacks and using them as opportunities to learn, improve, and push boundaries.

2. Oprah Winfrey, Media Mogul and Philanthropist: Oprah Winfrey faced numerous obstacles on her path to success, including a difficult childhood and early career setbacks. Despite these challenges, she persevered, remaining resilient and building a media empire that has made her one of the most influential and successful entrepreneurs in the world.

3. Jeff Bezos, Founder of Amazon: Jeff Bezos encountered countless obstacles while building Amazon into the global powerhouse it is today. From fierce competition to economic downturns, Bezos faced setbacks that could have deterred many entrepreneurs. However, his resilience and unwavering belief in his vision allowed him to weather the storms and transform Amazon into an e-commerce giant.

THE BENEFITS OF BUILDING RESILIENCE

Now, let's explore the specific benefits of building resilience as an entrepreneur:

1. Increased Mental and Emotional Well-being: Resilience enables you to better cope with stress, uncertainty, and the emotional rollercoaster of entrepreneurship. It helps you maintain a positive mindset, bounce back from failures, and protect your mental and emotional well-being.

2. Enhanced Problem-Solving and Adaptability: Resilience fosters the ability to think critically, adapt to changing circumstances, and find innovative solutions to problems. When faced with challenges, resilient entrepreneurs remain calm, analyze the situation, and find ways to navigate through obstacles.

3. Greater Perseverance and Determination: Building resilience fuels your perseverance and determination to continue pursuing your goals despite setbacks and obstacles. It instills a sense of purpose and the drive to keep pushing forward, even when faced with adversity.

4. Improved Decision-Making Skills: Resilient entrepreneurs have the ability to make sound decisions under pressure. They do not let setbacks or failures cloud their judgment but use them as opportunities to gather insights and make informed choices moving forward.

5. Increased Capacity for Risk-Taking: Resilience allows you to embrace calculated risks and step out of your comfort zone. It gives you the confidence to take bold actions, knowing that even if you encounter setbacks, you have the ability to bounce back and find alternative paths to success.

STRATEGIES FOR BUILDING RESILIENCE

Now, let's explore practical strategies for building resilience as an entrepreneur:

1. Develop a Growth Mindset: Cultivate a growth mindset that embraces challenges, learns from failures, and sees setbacks as opportunities for growth and learning.

2. Seek Support and Surround Yourself with a Strong Network: Build a support system of mentors, advisors, peers, and friends who can provide guidance, encouragement, and perspective during challenging times.

3. Practice Self-Care and Stress Management: Take care of your physical and mental well-being by practicing self-care activities such as exercise, mindfulness, and relaxation techniques. Managing stress effectively can help you maintain a clear and focused mindset during challenging periods.

4. Cultivate a Positive Mindset: Focus on the positive aspects of your journey, celebrate small wins, and reframe failures as learning experiences. Develop affirmations and positive self-talk to boost your confidence and resilience.

5. Learn from Setbacks and Adapt: View setbacks as opportunities to learn, adjust your strategies, and improve. Reflect on what went wrong, gather insights, and use them to pivot and adapt your approach moving forward.

CONCLUSION

In conclusion, resilience is a vital ingredient for entrepreneurial success. By cultivating a growth mindset and embracing challenges, setbacks, and failures as opportunities for growth, you develop the ability to bounce back and persevere in the face of adversity. The stories of Forbes 500 entrepreneurs serve as powerful reminders that resilience is not an innate trait but a skill that can be nurtured and strengthened through practice and determination.

Building resilience requires a shift in mindset. Instead of viewing failures as personal shortcomings, see them as valuable learning experiences that contribute to your growth and development. Embrace challenges as opportunities to stretch your abilities and refine your strategies. Recognize that setbacks are temporary and that with resilience, you can overcome them and continue on your entrepreneurial journey.

To cultivate resilience, it is important to develop a growth mindset. Believe in your ability to learn, adapt, and improve. Embrace a positive attitude and approach setbacks with a sense of curiosity and determination. Learn from your experiences, adjust your course when necessary, and keep moving forward.

Surrounding yourself with a supportive network is also crucial. Seek guidance and mentorship from experienced entrepreneurs who can provide valuable insights, encouragement, and support during challenging times. Connect with like-minded peers who share your drive for success and can offer fresh perspectives and encouragement along the way.

Taking care of your well-being is equally important. Entrepreneurship can be demanding and stressful, but prioritizing self-care helps you maintain your physical and mental health. Engage in activities that recharge your energy, practice mindfulness, and create balance in your life. By caring for yourself, you strengthen your resilience and enhance your ability to navigate the ups and downs of the entrepreneurial journey.

Remember, building resilience is a continuous process. It requires perseverance, self-reflection, and a commitment to personal growth. Embrace challenges, learn from setbacks, and let your resilience become the bedrock of your entrepreneurial journey. With resilience, you have the power to overcome obstacles, adapt to change, and ultimately achieve your goals and aspirations.

So, as you embark on your entrepreneurial path, nurture your resilience, embrace the growth mindset, and let your unwavering determination guide you. The journey may be challenging, but with resilience as your companion, you are equipped to overcome any obstacle and achieve extraordinary success. Your entrepreneurial dreams await—embrace the challenges, learn from setbacks, and let your resilience shine through.

6 CULTIVATING PERSISTENCE: STAYING THE COURSE

"Success is not the absence of failure; it's the persistence through failure." - Aisha Tyler

Welcome to Chapter 5 of "Unleash Your Inner Entrepreneur: The Power of the Growth Mindset." In this chapter, we delve into the importance of cultivating persistence as an entrepreneur and how it contributes to long-term success. Persistence is the ability to stay committed to your goals and objectives despite obstacles, setbacks, and challenges. By cultivating a growth mindset and developing persistence, you can navigate the unpredictable entrepreneurial journey with unwavering determination and achieve your vision.

THE ENTREPRENEURIAL JOURNEY: A TEST OF PERSISTENCE

The entrepreneurial journey is a test of persistence, requiring unwavering commitment and the ability to persevere in the face of challenges. It is a path filled with highs and lows, triumphs and failures. Successful entrepreneurs understand that setbacks and failures are not the end but opportunities for growth and learning.

Persistence is the fuel that keeps entrepreneurs going when the going gets tough. It is the mindset that propels them forward, even in the face of adversity and obstacles. Entrepreneurs who are persistent understand that success rarely comes overnight. It requires dedication, hard work, and a willingness to learn from mistakes.

The stories of Forbes 500 entrepreneurs are testament to the power of persistence. These individuals have faced numerous rejections and setbacks on their entrepreneurial journeys. They encountered failures, experienced doubts, and encountered roadblocks along the way. However, they refused to give up. They persisted, adapted their strategies, and remained resilient in the pursuit of their goals.

Persistence allows entrepreneurs to turn failures into stepping stones. Instead of being discouraged by setbacks, they view them as valuable learning experiences. Each failure brings them closer to success, as they learn important lessons, refine their approaches, and grow as individuals and business leaders.

The path to success is not linear, and there will inevitably be challenges and obstacles along the way. However, entrepreneurs who possess persistence are able to navigate these challenges with determination and resilience. They maintain a long-term perspective and remain focused on their goals, even when faced with setbacks or moments of doubt.

To cultivate persistence, it is important to develop a mindset of resilience and determination. Believe in your vision and the value of your work. Surround yourself with a supportive network of mentors, peers, and advisors who can offer guidance and encouragement during challenging times. Seek inspiration from the stories of successful entrepreneurs who have overcome obstacles and achieved great success through their persistence.

Additionally, embrace a growth mindset that allows you to view failures as opportunities for growth and learning. Learn from your mistakes, adapt your strategies, and keep pushing forward. Stay motivated by setting realistic goals and celebrating milestones along the way. Break down larger goals into smaller, achievable tasks, and take consistent action toward their accomplishment.

It's important to remember that persistence does not mean blindly sticking to a failing strategy. It requires the ability to adapt, learn from feedback, and make necessary adjustments. Persistence is not about stubbornly clinging to a single path but about having the resilience to persevere while remaining open to new possibilities and approaches.

In conclusion, the entrepreneurial journey is a test of persistence. It requires unwavering commitment, resilience, and the ability to persevere in the face of challenges. By embracing persistence, entrepreneurs can navigate the highs and lows of the journey and turn setbacks into opportunities for growth and learning. The stories of Forbes 500 entrepreneurs remind us that success is not achieved overnight but through perseverance, adaptability, and a relentless pursuit of one's goals. So, stay determined, stay focused, and let your persistence propel you towards entrepreneurial greatness.

THE GROWTH MINDSET AND PERSISTENCE

The growth mindset and persistence go hand in hand when it comes to entrepreneurial success. Entrepreneurs with a growth mindset understand that setbacks and failures are not indicative of their abilities or worth but are valuable learning experiences. They see challenges as opportunities for growth and improvement, which fuels their persistence in the face of adversity.

When faced with obstacles, entrepreneurs with a growth mindset don't shy away or give up easily. Instead, they view these challenges as an integral part of the entrepreneurial journey. They believe that their abilities and intelligence can be developed through effort, practice, and continuous learning. This mindset allows them to persist, adapt, and find alternative solutions when faced with roadblocks.

The stories of Forbes 500 entrepreneurs demonstrate the power of the growth mindset combined with persistence. These individuals have encountered numerous setbacks and failures, but their unwavering belief in their ability to learn and grow has kept them going. They view failures as stepping stones and use them as opportunities to gain new insights, refine their strategies, and ultimately move closer to their goals.

Entrepreneurs with a growth mindset and persistence don't let rejection or temporary setbacks define them. Instead, they see these experiences as feedback and motivation to continue pushing forward. They embrace a mindset of continuous improvement, always seeking ways to enhance their skills, expand their knowledge, and innovate in their respective industries.

To cultivate the growth mindset and persistence, it is important to reframe how you perceive setbacks and failures. Embrace a mindset of learning and growth, recognizing that these experiences provide valuable lessons that can contribute to your long-term success. Practice self-reflection to identify areas for improvement and seek feedback from mentors, peers, or customers to gain different perspectives.

Developing a resilient mindset is also essential. Entrepreneurship is filled with ups and downs, and setbacks are inevitable. By building resilience, you can bounce back from failures, setbacks, and rejections with a renewed sense of determination. Focus on your long-term goals, stay motivated, and remember that every step forward, no matter how small, is progress.

Surrounding yourself with a supportive network is equally important. Connect with like-minded individuals who share your drive for success and can provide encouragement, insights, and accountability along the way. Seek mentorship from experienced entrepreneurs who can offer guidance and share their own stories of persistence and growth.

In conclusion, the growth mindset and persistence are intertwined and essential for entrepreneurial success. By cultivating a growth mindset, you can embrace challenges, view setbacks as opportunities for growth, and persist in the face of adversity. The stories of Forbes 500 entrepreneurs serve as reminders that success is not achieved overnight but through a combination of a growth mindset, persistence, and a commitment to continuous learning. So, foster a growth mindset, embrace challenges, stay persistent, and let your entrepreneurial journey be guided by the belief that your potential is limitless.

REAL-LIFE EXAMPLES OF FORBES 500 ENTREPRENEURS

Let's draw inspiration from the stories of Forbes 500 entrepreneurs who have demonstrated remarkable persistence on their entrepreneurial journeys:

1. Mark Zuckerberg, Co-founder of Facebook: Mark Zuckerberg's journey with Facebook faced numerous challenges, including legal battles, privacy scandals, and fierce competition. However, his persistence in pursuing his vision of connecting the world has

enabled Facebook to become one of the most influential and successful companies in the world.

2. Sara Blakely, Founder of Spanx: Sara Blakely encountered numerous rejections from potential investors when she first introduced her innovative shapewear product, Spanx. However, her unwavering persistence and belief in her product led her to bootstrap her company, eventually building a billion-dollar business.

3. Richard Branson, Founder of Virgin Group: Richard Branson's entrepreneurial journey is marked by a series of ventures and failures. From failed record stores to unsuccessful airlines, Branson faced numerous setbacks. However, his persistence and ability to bounce back allowed him to build a diverse empire under the Virgin brand.

THE BENEFITS OF CULTIVATING PERSISTENCE

Now, let's explore the specific benefits of cultivating persistence as an entrepreneur:

1. Overcoming Challenges: Persistence allows you to overcome challenges and obstacles that come your way. It fuels your determination to find solutions, adapt your strategies, and keep moving forward, even when faced with adversity.

2. Learning from Failures: Persistence enables you to learn from failures and setbacks. It helps you view them as valuable lessons rather than reasons to give up. By persisting through failures, you gather insights, refine your approach, and increase your chances of success.

3. Building Resilience: Cultivating persistence builds resilience and mental strength. It helps you develop the ability to bounce back from failures, rejections, and disappointments, allowing you to maintain focus on your goals and push through challenging times.

4. Gaining Experience and Expertise: Persisting through challenges and setbacks allows you to gain valuable experience and expertise. Each hurdle you overcome provides you with valuable insights and knowledge that can be applied to future endeavors.

5. Achieving Long-Term Success: Persistence is often the key differentiator between those who achieve long-term success and those who give up too soon. By staying the course, remaining dedicated to your vision, and persisting through difficulties, you increase your chances of achieving your entrepreneurial goals.

STRATEGIES FOR CULTIVATING PERSISTENCE

Now, let's explore practical strategies for cultivating persistence as an entrepreneur:

1. Clarify Your Vision and Set Clear Goals: Clearly define your vision and set specific, measurable goals that align with your long-term vision. Having a clear direction helps you stay focused and motivated, even when faced with challenges.

2. Break Down Your Goals: Break down your big goals into smaller, manageable tasks. By focusing on bite-sized objectives, you can experience a sense of progress and achievement along the way, keeping your motivation and persistence high.

3. Develop a Strong Support System: Surround yourself with a network of supportive individuals who believe in you and your vision. Seek mentors, advisors, and like-minded peers who can provide guidance, encouragement, and accountability during challenging times.

4. Practice Resilience-Building Techniques: Engage in activities that build resilience, such as practicing mindfulness, self-reflection, and gratitude. Develop a positive mindset and cultivate resilience as a habit.

5. Celebrate Small Wins: Acknowledge and celebrate your achievements, no matter how small they may seem. Recognizing your progress boosts your confidence and motivation, fueling your persistence.

CONCLUSION

In conclusion, persistence is the key ingredient for success in the entrepreneurial journey. It is the unwavering commitment to your goals and the ability to persevere through challenges that sets successful entrepreneurs apart. By cultivating a growth mindset and embracing setbacks and failures as learning opportunities, you can develop the determination and resilience necessary to navigate the ups and downs of entrepreneurship.

The stories of Forbes 500 entrepreneurs serve as powerful reminders that persistence pays off. These individuals faced countless obstacles, rejections, and failures along their paths to success. However, they refused to give up. Instead, they used each setback as a stepping stone towards improvement, learning valuable lessons and gaining the experience necessary to push forward.

Cultivating persistence begins with developing a growth mindset. Embrace the belief that your abilities can be developed through dedication, effort, and continuous learning. See challenges as opportunities for growth and improvement rather than insurmountable barriers. Shift your perspective on failures, understanding that they are not indications of permanent shortcomings but stepping stones towards progress.

In the face of adversity, it is essential to stay committed to your goals. Understand that success is rarely achieved overnight and that the entrepreneurial journey is filled with ups and downs. Embrace a long-term perspective and stay focused on your vision. Celebrate small victories along the way and use them as motivation to keep going.

Resilience is a crucial aspect of persistence. Develop the ability to bounce back from failures and setbacks, learning from them and adapting your strategies as needed. Cultivate a positive mindset and surround yourself with a support network of mentors, peers, and like-minded individuals who can provide guidance and encouragement.

As you navigate the entrepreneurial journey, remember that persistence is not just about reaching your goals; it's about the growth and personal development you experience along the way. Embrace the challenges, setbacks, and failures as opportunities for self-improvement and learning. Let your persistence be the driving force that propels you forward, even when faced with adversity.

In conclusion, persistence is the fuel that keeps the entrepreneurial flame alive. It is the unwavering commitment, resilience, and growth mindset that enable entrepreneurs to overcome obstacles, learn from failures, and achieve their goals. The stories of Forbes 500 entrepreneurs serve as reminders that persistence is often the determining factor in entrepreneurial success. So, embrace persistence, stay focused on your vision, and let it guide you through the inevitable ups and downs of the entrepreneurial journey.

7 NURTURING A CULTURE OF INNOVATION: EMBRACING CREATIVITY AND CHANGE

"Innovation distinguishes between a leader and a follower." - Steve Jobs

Welcome to Chapter 7 of "Unleash Your Inner Entrepreneur: The Power of the Growth Mindset." In this chapter, we explore the importance of nurturing a culture of innovation within your entrepreneurial endeavors. Innovation is the driving force behind growth and success in today's rapidly evolving business landscape. By fostering a mindset that embraces creativity, change, and continuous improvement, you can create a dynamic environment that fuels innovation and propels your business forward.

THE ROLE OF INNOVATION IN ENTREPRENEURSHIP

Innovation is the lifeblood of entrepreneurship. It is the driving force that propels businesses forward, fuels growth, and sets successful entrepreneurs apart from the competition. In a rapidly changing business landscape, the ability to innovate is crucial for staying relevant, meeting customer needs, and creating a sustainable competitive advantage.

At its core, innovation is about identifying and seizing opportunities. Entrepreneurs with a keen eye for spotting gaps in the market or unmet customer needs can create products, services, or solutions that provide unique value. They have the vision to imagine what doesn't yet exist and the courage to bring it to life.

Innovation goes beyond mere invention. It involves the process of transforming ideas into tangible outcomes that make a difference. It requires creativity, problem-solving skills, and a willingness to take risks. Entrepreneurs who embrace innovation are not afraid to challenge the status quo, question assumptions, and explore new possibilities.

One of the key benefits of innovation is its ability to adapt to changing market trends. The business landscape is constantly evolving, driven by technological advancements, shifting consumer preferences, and emerging market forces. Entrepreneurs who stay ahead of the curve and proactively innovate are better positioned to meet these changes head-on. They can pivot their strategies, develop new products or services, and respond to customer demands effectively.

Moreover, innovation is a powerful tool for differentiation. In a crowded marketplace, where competition is fierce, standing out is crucial. By offering unique and innovative solutions, entrepreneurs can carve out a niche for themselves and attract customers who value the novelty and value they bring. Innovation allows entrepreneurs to create a distinctive brand identity, build customer loyalty, and establish themselves as leaders in their respective industries.

Innovation also fosters sustainable growth. By continuously innovating and improving their offerings, entrepreneurs can keep their businesses relevant and adaptable. They can uncover new revenue streams, expand into new markets, and secure a competitive advantage that is difficult to replicate. Innovation enables entrepreneurs to stay at the forefront of industry trends, anticipate customer needs, and position themselves as market leaders.

To foster a culture of innovation, entrepreneurs must create an environment that encourages and nurtures creativity. This includes fostering a growth mindset, embracing diversity of thought, and providing resources and support for experimentation. By empowering their teams to think outside the box, entrepreneurs can tap into the collective wisdom and ideas that drive innovation.

In conclusion, innovation is the heartbeat of entrepreneurship. It fuels growth, drives differentiation, and enables entrepreneurs to adapt to a rapidly changing business landscape. By embracing innovation, entrepreneurs can identify opportunities, develop unique solutions, and create sustainable competitive advantages. The stories of Forbes 500 entrepreneurs serve as reminders that innovation is not a luxury but a necessity in today's dynamic business world. So, embrace innovation, challenge the status quo, and let your entrepreneurial spirit shine through the power of innovation.

THE GROWTH MINDSET AND INNOVATION

The growth mindset and innovation go hand in hand, forming a powerful synergy that fuels entrepreneurial success. Entrepreneurs with a growth mindset possess the mindset and beliefs necessary to foster innovation within themselves and their organizations.

A growth mindset is characterized by the belief that abilities and intelligence can be developed through dedication, effort, and continuous learning. Entrepreneurs with a growth mindset see challenges, setbacks, and failures as opportunities for growth and improvement. They understand that failure is not a reflection of their abilities but a stepping stone towards success. This mindset allows them to approach innovation with a sense of curiosity, resilience, and adaptability.

Entrepreneurs with a growth mindset embrace new ideas and are open to different perspectives. They understand that innovation often requires thinking outside the box and challenging conventional wisdom. By being receptive to new ideas, they create an environment that encourages creativity, collaboration, and the exploration of uncharted territories.

Furthermore, entrepreneurs with a growth mindset are willing to take calculated risks. They understand that innovation inherently involves venturing into the unknown and that failure is a natural part of the process. Instead of fearing failure, they see it as a valuable learning experience that can provide insights and lessons for future endeavors. This willingness to take risks allows them to push the boundaries of what is possible and pursue innovative solutions with confidence.

A growth mindset also fosters resilience, which is crucial for innovation. Entrepreneurs with a growth mindset understand that the path to innovation is not always smooth. They are prepared to face obstacles, setbacks, and criticism along the way. However, their belief in their ability to learn and grow fuels their resilience and determination to persevere. They view challenges as opportunities to refine their ideas, iterate, and come back stronger.

Entrepreneurs with a growth mindset also prioritize continuous learning and personal development. They understand that innovation requires staying current with industry trends, advancements in technology, and emerging market forces. They seek out new knowledge, skills, and experiences to broaden their perspectives and enhance their ability to innovate. They are lifelong learners who embrace feedback and seek opportunities for growth and improvement.

By cultivating a growth mindset, entrepreneurs can create a culture of innovation within their organizations. They encourage their teams to adopt a growth mindset, embrace challenges, and take risks. They create an environment where diverse ideas are welcomed, experimentation is encouraged, and failure is seen as a stepping stone to success. This culture of innovation fuels creativity, fosters collaboration, and empowers individuals to unleash their full potential.

In conclusion, the growth mindset is a catalyst for innovation in entrepreneurship. Entrepreneurs with a growth mindset possess the mindset, beliefs, and behaviors that drive innovation and foster a culture of continuous improvement. By embracing challenges, taking risks, and nurturing a love for learning, they unleash their creative potential and drive transformative change. The stories of Forbes 500 entrepreneurs serve as reminders that the growth mindset is not just a mindset, but a powerful force that propels innovation and sets entrepreneurs on a path to extraordinary success. So, embrace the growth mindset, fuel your entrepreneurial spirit, and let innovation be the driving force that propels you towards greatness.

REAL-LIFE EXAMPLES OF FORBES 500 ENTREPRENEURS

Let's draw inspiration from the stories of Forbes 500 entrepreneurs who have nurtured a culture of innovation within their organizations:

1. Steve Jobs, Co-founder of Apple: Steve Jobs was known for his relentless pursuit of innovation. He fostered a culture at Apple that encouraged employees to think differently, take risks, and challenge

the status quo. This mindset of innovation led to the creation of revolutionary products like the iPhone, iPad, and Macintosh.

2. Reed Hastings, Co-founder of Netflix: Reed Hastings disrupted the traditional video rental industry by embracing innovation. He transformed Netflix from a DVD-by-mail service to a global streaming platform, recognizing the shift in consumer behavior and leveraging technology to deliver content in a new and convenient way.

3. Mary Barra, CEO of General Motors: Mary Barra transformed General Motors by instilling a culture of innovation and pushing the boundaries of traditional automotive manufacturing. Under her leadership, General Motors embraced electric vehicles, autonomous driving technology, and mobility services, positioning the company as a leader in the future of transportation.

THE BENEFITS OF NURTURING A CULTURE OF INNOVATION

Now, let's explore the specific benefits of nurturing a culture of innovation within your entrepreneurial endeavors:

1. Competitive Advantage: Innovation allows you to differentiate yourself from competitors by delivering unique products, services, or experiences. It gives you a competitive edge and positions your business as a leader in your industry.

2. Adaptability to Change: By embracing innovation, you develop the ability to adapt to changing market conditions, customer preferences, and technological advancements. This adaptability allows you to stay ahead of the curve and seize new opportunities.

3. Increased Efficiency and Productivity: Innovation often leads to improved processes, streamlined operations, and increased efficiency. By fostering a culture of innovation, you encourage employees to find creative solutions to challenges, which can result in cost savings, time efficiencies, and increased productivity.

4. Attraction and Retention of Talent: A culture of innovation attracts top talent who are eager to work in an environment that values creativity, experimentation, and continuous improvement. It fosters employee engagement, satisfaction, and retention, as individuals feel empowered to contribute their ideas and make a meaningful impact.

5. Business Growth and Expansion: Innovation is a catalyst for business growth. By continually seeking new opportunities, developing innovative products or services, and expanding into new markets, you can drive revenue growth and expand your entrepreneurial ventures.

STRATEGIES FOR NURTURING A CULTURE OF INNOVATION

Now, let's explore practical strategies for nurturing a culture of innovation within your entrepreneurial endeavors:

1. Encourage Idea Generation: Create platforms and spaces for employees to share their ideas, suggestions, and feedback. Foster a culture where all ideas are welcomed, and encourage open and transparent communication.

2. Foster Collaboration and Diversity: Encourage collaboration and diverse perspectives by fostering a culture of inclusion and respect. Embrace diversity in your teams, as different backgrounds, experiences, and viewpoints can lead to more innovative solutions.

3. Provide Resources and Support: Allocate resources and provide the necessary support for innovation initiatives. This includes providing training, access to technology, and dedicated time for employees to explore and develop new ideas.

4. Embrace Risk-Taking: Encourage calculated risk-taking by creating an environment where failure is seen as a learning opportunity rather than a source of punishment. Encourage employees to take calculated risks, experiment, and learn from both successes and failures.

5. Recognize and Reward Innovation: Celebrate and acknowledge innovative ideas, projects, or initiatives. Implement recognition and reward systems that encourage and motivate employees to contribute to innovation.

CONCLUSION

In conclusion, fostering a culture of innovation is a game-changer for entrepreneurial success. By embracing the growth mindset, entrepreneurs can create an environment that nurtures creativity, encourages risk-taking, and embraces change. This culture of innovation sets the stage for transformative breakthroughs, sustainable growth, and a competitive edge in the business landscape.

The growth mindset is the foundation of innovation. Entrepreneurs with a growth mindset believe that their abilities and intelligence can be developed through effort, practice, and continuous learning. They view challenges and setbacks as opportunities for growth, not as roadblocks. This mindset allows them to approach innovation with curiosity, resilience, and adaptability.

By fostering a growth mindset within themselves and their teams, entrepreneurs create a fertile ground for creativity to flourish. They encourage an open exchange of ideas, diverse perspectives, and constructive feedback. This creates a safe space for innovative thinking, where no idea is dismissed, and every voice is valued. Entrepreneurs with a growth mindset understand that innovation thrives in an environment that nurtures creativity, collaboration, and the freedom to think outside the box.

Embracing change is another essential aspect of fostering a culture of innovation. Entrepreneurs with a growth mindset understand that change is a constant in the business world. They are willing to embrace emerging trends, evolving customer needs, and disruptive technologies. They see change as an opportunity rather than a threat, and they adapt their strategies and approaches accordingly. This adaptability allows them to stay ahead of the curve and seize new possibilities.

Risk-taking is also inherent in the culture of innovation. Entrepreneurs with a growth mindset are not afraid to take calculated risks. They understand that innovation requires stepping outside of comfort zones and venturing into uncharted territories. They embrace the potential for failure and view it as a valuable learning experience. This willingness to take risks enables them to explore new opportunities, experiment with different approaches, and make bold moves that drive innovation.

Furthermore, entrepreneurs with a growth mindset prioritize continuous learning and personal development. They understand that to stay innovative, they need to stay curious and seek out new knowledge, insights, and skills. They invest in their own growth and that of their teams through training, mentorship, and networking. They encourage a culture of learning, where individuals are encouraged to expand their horizons, challenge assumptions, and stay at the forefront of their industries.

The stories of Forbes 500 entrepreneurs serve as powerful reminders that fostering a culture of innovation is not limited to tech giants or industry disruptors. Innovation can happen in any entrepreneurial venture, regardless of size or sector. It is the mindset, the beliefs, and the actions that matter. By embracing the growth mindset, entrepreneurs can ignite the spark of innovation, cultivate a culture that values creativity and change, and propel their ventures towards new heights of success.

In conclusion, nurturing a culture of innovation is not an option but a necessity for entrepreneurial success. By embracing the growth mindset, fostering creativity, embracing change, and encouraging risk-taking, entrepreneurs create an environment that fuels innovation and drives business growth. The stories of Forbes 500 entrepreneurs demonstrate the power of fostering a culture of innovation and the transformative impact it can have on entrepreneurial ventures. So, embrace the growth mindset, foster innovation, and let your entrepreneurial journey be defined by the pursuit of new possibilities, continuous improvement, and lasting success.

8 EMBRACING COLLABORATION: THE POWER OF BUILDING STRONG PARTNERSHIPS

"Alone we can do so little; together we can do so much." - Helen Keller

Welcome to Chapter 8 of "Unleash Your Inner Entrepreneur: The Power of the Growth Mindset." In this chapter, we delve into the importance of embracing collaboration and building strong partnerships in your entrepreneurial journey. Collaboration is a powerful tool that can propel your business to new heights, unlock opportunities, and foster innovation. By cultivating a growth mindset that values collaboration and seeks mutually beneficial partnerships, you can tap into the collective wisdom and resources of others to achieve shared success.

THE VALUE OF COLLABORATION IN ENTREPRENEURSHIP

In the world of entrepreneurship, collaboration is not just a buzzword; it is a powerful strategy for success. Collaborating with others allows entrepreneurs to tap into a diverse range of skills, expertise, and perspectives, propelling their ventures forward and opening doors to new opportunities.

One of the key benefits of collaboration is the ability to leverage complementary skills and knowledge. No entrepreneur is an expert in every aspect of business. By collaborating with others who have expertise in different areas, entrepreneurs can fill their knowledge gaps and strengthen their overall business acumen. For example, a tech-savvy entrepreneur may collaborate with a marketing expert to develop effective strategies for reaching their target audience. By pooling their expertise, they can create a more well-rounded and successful business.

Collaboration also offers the advantage of shared resources. In the entrepreneurial journey, resources such as funding, facilities, equipment, and networks can be limited. Through collaboration, entrepreneurs can access a broader pool of resources, sharing costs and maximizing their efficiency. For instance, two entrepreneurs in the same industry may collaborate to jointly purchase equipment or share office space, reducing expenses and enhancing their operational capabilities.

Beyond the practical benefits, collaboration fosters a culture of innovation and creativity. When individuals from different backgrounds and disciplines come together, fresh perspectives emerge, leading to the generation of new ideas and solutions. Collaborative environments encourage brainstorming, idea-sharing, and constructive feedback, creating an atmosphere where innovation can thrive. By collaborating with others, entrepreneurs can tap into a wealth of creativity, expanding the possibilities for their ventures.

Collaboration also extends to networking opportunities. Through collaboration, entrepreneurs can connect with like-minded individuals, potential partners, mentors, and investors. Building a strong network is crucial for entrepreneurial success, as it opens doors to new markets, partnerships, and resources. Collaborating with others allows entrepreneurs to tap into their networks, expanding their reach and unlocking valuable connections that can propel their ventures forward.

Furthermore, collaboration fosters a sense of camaraderie and support. Entrepreneurship can be a lonely journey, filled with ups and downs. By collaborating with others, entrepreneurs can find emotional support, motivation, and encouragement. Sharing challenges and triumphs with like-minded individuals who understand the entrepreneurial journey can provide a sense of community and boost morale during tough times. Collaborative relationships can also lead to long-term friendships and mutually beneficial partnerships that extend beyond the initial collaboration.

The stories of Forbes 500 entrepreneurs exemplify the value of collaboration in entrepreneurship. Many successful entrepreneurs attribute their achievements to strategic partnerships, mentorship, and collaboration with others. They recognize that collaboration enhances their capabilities, expands their networks, and accelerates their growth.

In conclusion, collaboration is not just a nice-to-have in entrepreneurship; it is a strategic imperative. By collaborating with others, entrepreneurs can leverage complementary skills, access shared resources, foster innovation, expand their networks, and find support along their entrepreneurial journey. The stories of Forbes 500 entrepreneurs serve as inspiring examples of the power of collaboration in driving business success. So, embrace collaboration, seek out opportunities to collaborate with others, and let the collective power of collaboration propel your entrepreneurial venture to new heights of achievement.

THE GROWTH MINDSET AND COLLABORATION

The growth mindset and collaboration go hand in hand in the world of entrepreneurship. Entrepreneurs with a growth mindset understand that they are not limited by their own knowledge and abilities, but rather, they can learn and grow by collaborating with others who bring different skills and expertise to the table.

One of the key aspects of the growth mindset is the belief that talents and abilities can be developed through dedication, effort, and continuous learning. Entrepreneurs with a growth mindset see collaboration as an opportunity to learn from others and expand their own knowledge and capabilities. They understand that by working with individuals who have different strengths and expertise, they can acquire new skills, gain fresh perspectives, and enhance their overall entrepreneurial toolkit.

Collaboration also aligns with the growth mindset because it challenges the notion that success is achieved solely through individual effort. Entrepreneurs with a growth mindset recognize that collaboration allows them to achieve more than they could on their own. By leveraging the collective knowledge, skills, and resources of a collaborative team, they can tackle complex challenges, explore innovative solutions, and achieve greater outcomes.

Furthermore, the growth mindset encourages entrepreneurs to embrace feedback and see it as an opportunity for growth. Collaboration inherently involves giving and receiving feedback, as team members provide insights, suggestions, and constructive criticism to one another. Entrepreneurs with a growth mindset value this feedback as a means to improve their own performance, refine their ideas, and enhance their entrepreneurial endeavors.

Collaboration also fosters a culture of innovation, which is a core principle of the growth mindset. By bringing together individuals with diverse backgrounds, experiences, and perspectives, collaboration encourages the generation of new ideas and the exploration of alternative approaches. Entrepreneurs with a growth mindset see collaboration as a way to fuel creativity, challenge assumptions, and push the boundaries of what is possible.

The growth mindset also supports the development of strong relationships and networks, which are crucial for entrepreneurial success. Entrepreneurs with a growth mindset understand the value of building connections with others who can offer support, guidance, and partnership. Through collaboration, entrepreneurs can expand their networks, establish mutually beneficial relationships, and tap into new opportunities for growth and advancement.

The stories of Forbes 500 entrepreneurs demonstrate the power of the growth mindset and collaboration. Many successful entrepreneurs attribute their achievements to collaborative efforts, strategic partnerships, and the collective power of working together towards a common goal. They recognize that collaboration enhances their own capabilities, fosters innovation, and accelerates their entrepreneurial growth.

In conclusion, the growth mindset and collaboration are intertwined in the entrepreneurial journey. By embracing collaboration, entrepreneurs with a growth mindset can tap into the collective knowledge, skills, and resources of a collaborative team, learn from others, foster innovation, and achieve greater outcomes. The stories of Forbes 500 entrepreneurs serve as inspiring examples of the synergy between the growth mindset and collaboration in driving entrepreneurial success. So, adopt a growth mindset, seek out collaborative opportunities, and let the power of collaboration propel your entrepreneurial venture to new heights of achievement.

REAL-LIFE EXAMPLES OF FORBES 500 ENTREPRENEURS

Let's draw inspiration from the stories of Forbes 500 entrepreneurs who have embraced collaboration and built strong partnerships:

1. Jeff Bezos, Founder of Amazon: Jeff Bezos understood the power of collaboration from the early days of Amazon. He built a robust ecosystem of partnerships with suppliers, sellers, and logistics providers, creating a seamless experience for customers and fueling Amazon's exponential growth.

2. Indra Nooyi, Former CEO of PepsiCo: Indra Nooyi transformed PepsiCo by fostering collaboration with various stakeholders. She engaged with employees, customers, and partners to drive innovation, develop sustainable practices, and expand PepsiCo's product portfolio.

3. Elon Musk, CEO of Tesla and SpaceX: Elon Musk's success can be attributed, in part, to his ability to form strategic partnerships. From collaboration with other automakers to co-developing technologies with NASA, Musk has leveraged partnerships to accelerate innovation and achieve his ambitious goals.

THE BENEFITS OF EMBRACING COLLABORATION

Now, let's explore the specific benefits of embracing collaboration within your entrepreneurial endeavors:

1. Access to Expertise and Resources: Collaboration allows you to tap into the expertise, knowledge, and resources of others. By partnering with individuals or organizations who possess complementary skills or assets, you can leverage their strengths to enhance your entrepreneurial ventures.

2. Accelerated Innovation: Collaboration brings together diverse perspectives, experiences, and ideas, fostering an environment that sparks innovation. By collaborating with others, you can co-create new products, services, or solutions that have a broader impact and resonate with your target market.

3. Expanded Networks and Opportunities: Collaborating with others expands your network and opens doors to new opportunities. Through partnerships, you can access new markets, reach new customers, and establish connections with influential individuals or organizations that can propel your entrepreneurial ventures forward.

4. Shared Risk and Support: When you collaborate, you share both the risks and rewards. By working together, you can navigate challenges more effectively, share the burden of uncertainty, and provide support to one another, increasing the likelihood of success.

5. Enhanced Brand and Reputation: Collaborating with reputable and respected partners can enhance your brand and reputation. By associating with trusted partners, you gain credibility and build trust with customers, stakeholders, and the wider business community.

STRATEGIES FOR EMBRACING COLLABORATION

Now, let's explore practical strategies for embracing collaboration within your entrepreneurial endeavors:

1. Identify Complementary Partners: Identify individuals, organizations, or businesses that possess complementary skills, knowledge, or resources that align with your entrepreneurial goals. Look for partners who share your values, vision, and commitment to growth.

2. Foster Relationships and Trust: Build relationships based on trust, open communication, and mutual respect. Take the time to understand your potential partners' goals, challenges, and aspirations, and seek to create mutually beneficial outcomes.

3. Establish Clear Objectives and Expectations: Clearly define the objectives, roles, and responsibilities of each partner involved in the collaboration. Establish expectations around communication, decision-making, and accountability to ensure a smooth and productive collaboration.

4. Promote Knowledge Sharing and Learning: Create opportunities for knowledge sharing and learning within the collaborative partnership. Encourage the exchange of ideas, best practices, and lessons learned to foster continuous improvement and growth.

5. Nurture Long-Term Relationships: Collaboration is not a one-time event but an ongoing process. Invest in building long-term relationships with your partners by demonstrating commitment, delivering on promises, and finding ways to create value for all involved.

CONCLUSION

In conclusion, collaboration is a cornerstone of entrepreneurial success. By adopting a growth mindset that embraces collaboration, entrepreneurs can tap into the collective wisdom, skills, and resources of others to accelerate their journey towards achieving their goals. The stories of Forbes 500 entrepreneurs illustrate the transformative power of collaboration in driving growth, fostering innovation, and achieving market leadership.

When entrepreneurs cultivate a growth mindset that values collaboration, they recognize that they don't have to go it alone. They understand that by working together with others who bring diverse perspectives, skills, and experiences, they can achieve far more than they could on their own. Collaboration allows entrepreneurs to leverage the strengths of their team members, complement their own skill sets, and access a broader range of resources and expertise.

Moreover, collaboration aligns with the growth mindset by encouraging a continuous learning mindset. Entrepreneurs who collaborate with others are open to new ideas, receptive to feedback, and willing to adapt and evolve. They see collaboration as an opportunity to expand their knowledge, gain fresh insights, and refine their approaches. By embracing collaboration, entrepreneurs can foster a culture of learning and improvement within their entrepreneurial ventures.

Collaboration also sparks innovation. When individuals with different backgrounds, perspectives, and expertise come together, they can generate creative solutions, challenge conventional thinking, and drive breakthrough innovation. Collaborative environments encourage the exchange of ideas, the exploration of diverse approaches, and the cross-pollination of knowledge, all of which are essential for entrepreneurial success in today's rapidly changing business landscape.

The stories of Forbes 500 entrepreneurs serve as powerful examples of the impact of collaboration. Many of these entrepreneurs attribute their success to strategic partnerships, collaborative efforts, and the collective power of working together towards a common goal. They understand that collaboration can lead to exponential growth, increased market share, and sustainable competitive advantages.

By embracing collaboration, entrepreneurs can also build strong networks and relationships. Collaboration opens doors to new connections, expands professional networks, and fosters mutually beneficial partnerships. These relationships can provide access to new opportunities, mentorship, and support, further fueling entrepreneurial growth and success.

In conclusion, embracing collaboration is a powerful strategy for entrepreneurial success. By cultivating a growth mindset that values collaboration, seeking out strategic partnerships, and leveraging the collective wisdom and resources of others, entrepreneurs can amplify their impact and achieve shared success. The stories of Forbes 500 entrepreneurs demonstrate the transformative power of collaboration in driving growth, fostering innovation, and achieving market leadership. So, embrace collaboration, build strong partnerships, and let the collective efforts of like-minded individuals propel your entrepreneurial endeavors to new heights. Together, we can achieve remarkable things.

CONCLUSION

Congratulations! You have reached the final chapter of "Unleash Your Inner Entrepreneur: The Power of the Growth Mindset." Throughout this book, we have explored strategies for cultivating a growth mindset in business and witnessed the transformative impact it can have on your entrepreneurial journey. From understanding the power of mindset to embracing challenges, nurturing resilience, and leveraging collaboration and innovation, you have gained valuable insights and practical tools to unlock your full potential as an entrepreneur.

THE GROWTH MINDSET AS A FOUNDATION

The growth mindset serves as a solid foundation for your entrepreneurial endeavors. It is the belief that abilities and intelligence can be developed through dedication, effort, and continuous learning. By adopting a growth mindset, you can overcome self-limiting beliefs, embrace challenges, and persevere through obstacles on your path to success.

In the early stages of your entrepreneurial journey, it is essential to cultivate a growth mindset to navigate the uncertainties and setbacks that inevitably arise. By reframing failures as opportunities for growth and viewing challenges as stepping stones to success, you can maintain a positive outlook and keep moving forward, even in the face of adversity.

THE POWER OF MINDSET SHIFTS

As an entrepreneur, you have the power to shift your mindset and transform your approach to business. Throughout this book, we have explored mindset shifts that can lead to exponential growth and success. By embracing a growth mindset, you can:

1. Embrace Challenges: Rather than avoiding challenges, you can view them as opportunities for growth and learning. By stepping outside your comfort zone and taking on new and exciting challenges, you can expand your skills, knowledge, and capabilities as an entrepreneur.

2. Cultivate Resilience: Resilience is the ability to bounce back from setbacks and persevere in the face of adversity. By cultivating resilience, you can navigate the inevitable ups and downs of entrepreneurship and maintain a steadfast commitment to your goals.

3. Leverage Failure as Feedback: Failure is not the end; it is merely feedback on your journey to success. By reframing failure as an opportunity to learn, adapt, and improve, you can turn setbacks into stepping stones toward greater achievements.

4. Embrace Continuous Learning: Entrepreneurship is a constant learning process. By adopting a growth mindset, you recognize that there is always more to learn and discover. Embrace a thirst for knowledge, seek out new experiences, and remain open to learning from others.

THE STORIES OF FORBES 500 ENTREPRENEURS

The stories of Forbes 500 entrepreneurs have served as beacons of inspiration and guidance throughout this book. We have seen how some of the world's most successful entrepreneurs have cultivated a growth mindset and applied its principles to their business ventures.

From the visionary leadership of Steve Jobs, who transformed Apple into a technology giant through relentless innovation, to the strategic partnerships forged by Elon Musk, who leveraged collaboration to achieve groundbreaking milestones in electric vehicles and space exploration, these stories remind us that the growth mindset is a driving force behind entrepreneurial success.

By studying the mindsets and strategies of Forbes 500 entrepreneurs, we have gained valuable insights into the practical applications of the growth mindset. We have seen how these entrepreneurs approached challenges, adapted to change, and harnessed their inner drive to create transformative businesses that have reshaped industries and touched the lives of millions.

APPLYING THE GROWTH MINDSET TO YOUR ENTREPRENEURIAL JOURNEY

As you conclude your journey through this book, it is essential to reflect on how you can apply the principles of the growth mindset to your own entrepreneurial journey. Here are some key takeaways to consider:

1. Embrace a Growth Mindset: Adopt a mindset that embraces challenges, growth, and continuous learning. Believe in your ability to learn, develop new skills, and overcome obstacles along the way.

2. Cultivate Resilience: Develop resilience by reframing setbacks as opportunities for growth. Embrace setbacks as learning experiences and use them to fuel your determination to succeed.

3. Seek Feedback and Learn from Failure: Embrace failure as a stepping stone to success. Use failures as opportunities to learn, adapt, and improve your entrepreneurial ventures.

4. Embrace Collaboration and Innovation: Recognize the power of collaboration and the value of diverse perspectives. Seek out partnerships and collaborations that can fuel innovation, accelerate growth, and create new opportunities.

5. Stay Curious and Continuously Learn: Maintain a curious mindset and a thirst for knowledge. Seek out new experiences, stay informed about industry trends, and be open to learning from others.

Remember, building a growth mindset is not a one-time event but an ongoing journey. It requires dedication, commitment, and a willingness to challenge your own beliefs and assumptions. As you continue on your entrepreneurial path, remember that your mindset will determine your level of success and fulfillment.

CLOSING THOUGHTS

In "Unleash Your Inner Entrepreneur: The Power of the Growth Mindset," we have explored the mindset shifts, strategies, and real-life examples that can empower you to achieve entrepreneurial greatness. The growth mindset is not a magical solution, but rather a powerful tool that, when wielded with intention and determination, can transform your entrepreneurial journey.

As you embark on your path as an entrepreneur, embrace the growth mindset and let it guide your decisions, actions, and interactions. Believe in your ability to learn, adapt, and create positive change. Embrace challenges, foster resilience, and collaborate with others to unlock new possibilities and achieve remarkable results.

Now is the time to unleash your inner entrepreneur, armed with the power of the growth mindset. Embrace the journey, celebrate the milestones, and let your entrepreneurial endeavors leave a lasting impact on the world. The future is yours for the taking.

ABOUT THE AUTHOR

"Learn, learn and learn. Once you stop learning everything stops" - Engin Yokaribas

Engin Yokaribas, a seasoned entrepreneur and digital strategist, is a visionary in the world of online business. With a proven track record of building successful ventures and helping businesses achieve remarkable growth, Engin is a trusted authority in the field of entrepreneurship and digital marketing.

Throughout Engin's career, he has demonstrated a keen understanding of the online landscape and a knack for identifying lucrative opportunities. He has successfully built multiple online businesses from the ground up, leveraging his expertise to navigate the competitive online marketplace and achieve exceptional results.

Beyond his own ventures, Engin has played a pivotal role in helping numerous businesses achieve 7-8 figure growth. his strategic insights, innovative approaches, and tailored strategies have consistently delivered measurable results, catapulting businesses to new heights of success.

With a passion for sharing knowledge and empowering aspiring entrepreneurs, Engin is dedicated to helping others unlock their full potential in the digital realm. He believes in the transformative power of entrepreneurship and is committed to providing invaluable insights, proven strategies, and practical advice to help readers navigate the complexities of launching and growing a profitable online business.

As a sought-after speaker and consultant, Engin has inspired audiences and worked closely with businesses across diverse industries. His hands-on experience, combined with a deep understanding of the digital landscape, allows him to offer practical guidance that is grounded in real-world success.

Whether you are a budding entrepreneur seeking guidance or an established business owner looking to make your mark in the digital world, Engin's expertise and wisdom will equip you with the tools and mindset needed to thrive in the dynamic landscape of online entrepreneurship.

Embark on this transformative journey with Engin Yokaribas as your trusted guide, and unlock the secrets to building a profitable online empire that surpasses your wildest dreams.